Fish in the Dark

Fish in the Dark

Larry David

Grove Press
New York

Printed in the United States of America

FIRST EDITION

ISBN 978-0-8021-2440-1
eISBN 978-0-8021-9128-1

Grove Press
an imprint of Grove Atlantic
154 West 14th Street
New York, NY 10011

Distributed by Publishers Group West

groveatlantic.com

15 16 17 18   10 9 8 7 6 5 4 3 2 1

PRODUCTION CREDITS

Fish in the Dark received its world premiere at the Cort Theatre on Broadway, with previews beginning on February 2 and opening on March 5, 2015. The production was directed by Anna D. Shapiro. Todd Rosenthal, Scenic Design; Ann Roth, Costume Design; Brian MacDevitt, Lighting Design; Rob Milburn and Michael Bodeen, Sound Design; Alan D'Angerio, Wig Design; Caparelliotis Casting, Casting; Rolt Smith, Production Stage Manager; Penelope Daulton, Company Manager; Aurora Productions, Production Management; Philip Rinaldi, Press Representative; Van Dyke Parks, Original Music. *Fish in the Dark* was originally produced on the stage by Scott Rudin, Lloyd Braun, Eli Bush, Roger Berlind, William Berlind, Roy Furman, Jon B. Platt, Ruth Hendel, the Shubert Organization, Catherine and Fred Adler, Jay Alix and Una Jackman, Scott M. Delman, Jean Doumanian, Sonia Friedman, Tulchin Bartner Productions, Heni Koenigsberg, Daryl Roth, True Love Productions. Executive Producers: Joey Parnes, Sue Wagner, John Johnson. The cast was as follows:

Norman	Larry David
Brenda	Rita Wilson
Arthur	Ben Shenkman
Michelle	Jenn Lyon
Doctor Stiles	Richard Topol
Gloria	Jayne Houdyshell
Fabiana	Rosie Perez
Natalie	Molly Ranson
Greg	Jonny Orsini
Rose	Marylouise Burke
Harry	Kenneth Tigar
Stewie	Lewis J. Stadlen
Sidney	Jerry Adler

Nurse	Maria Elena Ramirez
Jay Leventhal	Jeff Still
Jessica	Rachel Resheff
Diego	Jake Cannavale
Doctor Meyers	Joel Rooks

CHARACTERS

NORMAN DREXEL
Early to mid-50s, average in every respect except for his hyperactive libido.

BRENDA DREXEL
A few years younger than Norman; honest, cheery, and optimistic, all qualities sorely lacking in her husband.

ARTHUR DREXEL
Norman's brother, two years younger than him; much wealthier, better-looking, and divorced.

MICHELLE
A voluptuous, full-of-life blonde who is dating Arthur and works as a notary for their father's lawyer.

DOCTOR STILES
A doctor at the hospital where Sidney is staying.

GLORIA
Mother of Norman and Arthur, early to mid-70s, bad wig and all.

FABIANA
Puerto Rican housekeeper at Norman and Brenda's house, early 40s.

NATALIE
Norman and Brenda's daughter, early 20s.

GREG
Natalie's goofy boyfriend.

ROSE
Sidney's sister.

HARRY
Rose's husband.

STEWIE
Sidney's blustery, bull-in-a-china-shop younger brother.

SIDNEY
Norman and Arthur's father, now dying in hospital.

NURSE
A nurse at the hospital.

JAY LEVENTHAL
Lawyer and estate planner to Sidney, and employer of Michelle, in his mid-50s.

JESSICA
Arthur's precocious fourteen-year-old daughter.

DIEGO
Fabiana's son, young and handsome.

DOCTOR MEYERS
Gloria's doctor at the hospital.

Fish in the Dark

ACT ONE

We open on a darkened stage. It's the middle of the night and a couple,
NORMAN and BRENDA DREXEL, are fast asleep.

Norman, early to mid-50s, average in every respect, except for his
hyperactive libido, which, due to the exigencies of marriage, is hardly
a blessing. Brenda is a few years younger than Norman. She's honest,
cheery, and optimistic, all qualities sorely lacking in her husband.

After a few beats, the ringing of a phone breaks the silence.

The scene is played in the dark with voiceovers.

NORMAN (*bolting awake*)   Oh my God! Who's dead?!

BRENDA   Answer it, Norman.

NORMAN   Someone died! Someone's dead!

BRENDA   Pick up the phone.

NORMAN   Someone's dead. I know it. (*picks up the phone*)
. . . Hello? . . . What's wrong? Uh-huh . . . uh-huh . . . Should I
come now? Oh . . . Okay, then I'll see you in the morning. Okay,
bye. (*he hangs up*) That was Arthur. They took my father to the
hospital. Same issue with the breathing. I have a feeling this might
be it. I'll go first thing in the morning.

BRENDA   Are you okay?

NORMAN   I don't understand.

BRENDA   . . . Well he's old and sick. We knew this was coming.

3

NORMAN   I mean, if we can't go until the morning, why did Arthur wake us? How does waking us at three am do anything?

BRENDA   It doesn't. It's all about, "If I'm up, you're up".

NORMAN   Yeah, of course. Well, I'll tell you this. There's no way I can get back to bed now.

BRENDA   What do you want to do?

NORMAN   Well this is going to sound like a joke, but usually in circumstances like these, there's really only one thing that gets me back to bed.

BRENDA   Really?

NORMAN   Absolutely. It completely changes the sleep dynamic.

BRENDA   You can still do that, even with what happened to your father?

NORMAN   Especially so.

BRENDA   . . . So would you prefer I leave the room or should I just turn around?

NORMAN (*deflated*)   . . . You can just turn around.

BRENDA   Enjoy.

   Blackout

The lights come up on a hospital visitors' lounge. There's a vinyl couch CS, with two brightly colored plastic chairs on either side. DL are a candy and coffee machine. Two sets of elevators are UC.

Norman exits his father SIDNEY's room, DR, and approaches Brenda, who's sitting on the couch, checking her cell.

NORMAN   No change. Still sleeping.

BRENDA   Natalie's on her way. She's coming from her *My Fair Lady* rehearsal. How are you doing? Can I get you anything?

NORMAN   You know what I just realized? Except for when I was born, I have never spent a night in the hospital in my life. I'm Superman.

BRENDA   If I were you, I'd knock on wood.

NORMAN (*looking around*)   Oh my God, there's no wood. That's not wood. That's fake wood.

BRENDA (*points to end table*)   That's wood.

NORMAN   That's not wood. That's fake wood. It's faux wood! This is all faux!

BRENDA   You can knock on faux wood.

NORMAN   Ah, you don't know what the faux you're talking about.

The elevator doors open, revealing Norman's brother, ARTHUR DREXEL. He's two years younger than Norman, much wealthier, better-looking, and enjoying the divorced life. The shirt, however, is not coming off his back for anyone. Arthur is accompanied by MICHELLE, a voluptuous, full-of-life blonde. Arthur hugs Brenda.

ARTHUR   Hey! This is Michelle. Michelle, this is my brother's wife, Brenda—

BRENDA   —Your sister-in-law.

ARTHUR   Right. And this is my brother, Norman.

Norman gives a nod of approval to Arthur regarding Michelle.

MICHELLE   Hello. Sorry about your dad.

NORMAN   Thanks, but you know what? In a way it's a relief. He's been suffering for a while.

MICHELLE   I get that.

NORMAN   Wait a second! You work with Jay Leventhal. You're the notary, right?

MICHELLE   Right.

NORMAN   Sure, I met you a few years ago. I was up in the office.

MICHELLE   I remember.

NORMAN   You remember! She remembers!

Brenda claps sarcastically.

ARTHUR   Have you seen Dad?

NORMAN   Just briefly.

ARTHUR   Where's Mom?

NORMAN   She went to get some food.

ARTHUR   How's she doing?

NORMAN   Well she hasn't been rendered mute, if that's what you're asking.

BRENDA   It would have to be a catastrophe of biblical proportions for that to happen.

ARTHUR (*to Michelle*)   Pick a date. Any date in the last forty years.

BRENDA   Seriously?

ARTHUR (*ignoring, to Michelle*)   Name one.

MICHELLE (*confused*)   Um . . . November 25, 1997.

BRENDA   It was the Tuesday before Thanksgiving. I opened the
door for the paper, but it hadn't been delivered. Then I had a
sesame seed bagel. I dunked it in my coffee, which Norman didn't
like at all.

NORMAN   You don't dunk bagels. Who dunks bagels? Goyim.

BRENDA   Then my cousin called. I tried handing Norman
the phone so he could wish her a happy Thanksgiving, but he
refused to take it. (*unflattering imitation of Norman*) "No! No! No!
I can't!"

NORMAN   Oh, wow, what a great impression. You really got me
down.

MICHELLE (*in awe, to Brenda*)   . . . How do you know that?

ARTHUR   She can remember where she was and what she did
every day since she was five. Only thirteen people in the world
can do it.

MICHELLE   That's incredible.

NORMAN   I don't like being handed phones. Lotta pressure for
me.

ARTHUR (*to Michelle*)   Yes, they're an interesting couple, these
two. The idiot and the savant.

NORMAN (*to Arthur, gesturing to Sidney's room*)   You want to go in
to see your father maybe? Just a suggestion.

Norman waits for Arthur and Michelle to enter Sidney's room, then:

She's going in? What the hell is that? He brings a date to the
hospital? His father's dying and he brings a date?

BRENDA   Maybe she's not a date. Maybe she's a girlfriend.

7

NORMAN   She's not a girlfriend. I spoke to him last week. He didn't mention anything about a girlfriend. I'm not even sure if a girlfriend is appropriate here.

BRENDA   I wish I could've seen you guys together when you were kids.

NORMAN   Oh, it was much worse. I used to pin him down and drool until it was an inch from his face, then suck it back up.

BRENDA (*wincing*)   Eww . . .

NORMAN   Yeah, it was pretty disgusting. I think he's still getting even.

ARTHUR (*interrupting*)   He's tired, said he wasn't up for talking.

BRENDA   Where's Michelle?

ARTHUR   She's using the bathroom. She wants to take her contacts out.

BRENDA   Anybody care for real coffee? I'm going out.

NORMAN   No thanks.

   Brenda exits.

So how long have you been seeing her?

ARTHUR   This is our fourth date.

NORMAN   So this is a date?

ARTHUR   Well it's the fourth time we're getting together. Technically, the first ten times you see a new woman, it's a date. So yeah.

NORMAN   This is wildly inappropriate. I hate to inform you, but the deathbed is not the place to meet new people. It's not a mixer. Why is she here?

   DOCTOR STILES enters.

DR. STILES (*to Norman*) Is this your brother?

NORMAN Yes. Arthur, this is Dr. Stiles.

ARTHUR (*to Norman*) Do I really have to explain it? I didn't know what time I'd be getting out of here—

NORMAN I have no idea what you're talking about.

ARTHUR . . . It's just more convenient. Logistics.

To Dr. Stiles.

Dr. Stiles, pleasure. So what's going on? What is it, the carbon dioxide?

DR. STILES Exactly. He's only using five percent of his lung capacity and, as a result, there's an accumulation of CO_2 because his lungs can't get rid of it. To be absolutely truthful, I'm sorry, but I don't expect him to last more than a day or two . . . unless . . .

ARTHUR What?

DR. STILES Unless we put him on a ventilator.

ARTHUR A ventilator?

DR. STILES It would keep him alive, but he could never recover.

NORMAN Problem is, he never made any provisions for a ventilator. Someone would have to ask him.

Awkward pause. He turns to Dr. Stiles.

. . . So what do you think?

DR. STILES About what?

NORMAN You know . . . asking him.

DR. STILES About the ventilator?

NORMAN Yeah.

DR. STILES Well, you're his son. You should do it.

NORMAN   You're a doctor. Kind of your job.

DR. STILES   Yeah, maybe if you two weren't here.

ARTHUR   We'll go get a bite.

NORMAN   We'll bring you back a little something.

ARTHUR   What do you like?

NORMAN   We'll go get a bite . . . You'll have your ventilator talk. We'll come back with a delicious lunch.

DR. STILES   I think not.

ARTHUR   Okay, so what happens if nobody asks him?

DR. STILES   Then we put him on one and keep him alive . . . Let me know what you decide. Nice to meet you. (*he exits*)

ARTHUR   You believe that?

NORMAN   What kind of doctor is this? It's way easier for him to ask. He must have a lot of ventilator talks. We've had no ventilator talks.

ARTHUR   I know. We have no ventilator experience.

NORMAN   Zero! We have zero ventilator experience! So . . . I guess we should flip a coin for who asks.

ARTHUR   No. I can't do it. Sorry, Norman. I cannot go in there and ask Dad that. Please.

NORMAN   You think I want to? I can't ask him. The fair way is to flip.

ARTHUR   Yes, I realize that would be the fair way.

NORMAN   So you'd rather let your father languish on a ventilator than ask him?

ARTHUR   Yes, I would.

NORMAN   So I have to do it?

ARTHUR He should've had this all worked out ahead of time.

NORMAN I know. Like what about the body? I guess we need a mortician.

ARTHUR Where do we get that?

NORMAN Google? Yelp? I don't know.

ARTHUR How much is a casket?

NORMAN A thousand, two thousand?

ARTHUR I'll tell you right now, I'm not spending more than five hundred on a casket. Who cares what he's buried in? It's not a house. He's not living there.

NORMAN I don't want my father buried in some shithole.

ARTHUR Why? He doesn't know where he is.

NORMAN Okay, this is a ridiculous argument.

ARTHUR Why should anyone care where they're buried? You could throw me in a garbage dump. Doesn't matter. I'm dead.

NORMAN Okay, so if you die before me, I can throw you in a garbage dump?

ARTHUR Absolutely. Right in the dumpster.

NORMAN Oh I cannot wait for your funeral! That is going to be fun. We'll all drive to the garbage dump.

ARTHUR You know what? I have a better idea. Maybe we should cremate him. We'll all save a ton of money. A cremation costs nothing.

NORMAN Boy, for a guy with a lot of money, you're so cheap.

ARTHUR Not a ton.

NORMAN Oh, it's a ton.

ARTHUR   That has nothing to do with it. It's the principle. Why should the living sacrifice for the dead? You don't spend on the dead. Nothing for the dead. They get nothing!

The elevator doors open and GLORIA DREXEL, their mother, early to mid-70s, bad wig and all, makes her entrance. You don't want to get on Gloria's bad side, but unfortunately that's not an option.

GLORIA *(happy to see her son)*   Oh, Arthur.

They hug.

ARTHUR   He had a good life, Mom.

GLORIA   What was so good about it?

NORMAN   It wasn't so good? I thought it was good.

GLORIA   It was okay. That floor in the lobby is so slippery, I almost broke my neck. They don't need to put so much wax on it. Just mop it. It's not the White House!

ARTHUR   Mom, did you ever talk to Dad about going on a ventilator?

GLORIA   I did. He said if he ever couldn't eat or maintain his hygiene, he'd rather die.

ARTHUR   Well that settles that.

GLORIA   And Tony Severino called. Said he wants to come and say good-bye to Dad, but I told him no.

She opens the door to Sidney's room and then closes it immediately, jolted.

NORMAN   What happened?

GLORIA   Nothing.

ARTHUR   Mom? Mom, what happened?

GLORIA   Nothing! Nothing happened!

NORMAN Mom! What?

GLORIA Your father was feeling up some girl!

NORMAN What?

ARTHUR Michelle?

GLORIA A blonde woman.

ARTHUR Oh my God!

He goes back into Sidney's room.

NORMAN Where was he touching her?

GLORIA You have to know where?

NORMAN I'm just curious.

GLORIA Her breasts, okay? He was touching her breasts!

NORMAN Wow.

GLORIA Who is this girl?

NORMAN I don't know. Arthur's date.

GLORIA His date? Your brother is some idiot. He brings a strange girl to the hospital? And what about your father? How do you explain that?

NORMAN Sometimes the hand wants what the hand wants.

Arthur and Michelle return.

ARTHUR Mom, this is . . .

And before Arthur can get her name out, Gloria walks past them and back into Sidney's room. To Michelle:

Oh my God. Is it true?

MICHELLE It's true.

NORMAN How did it happen?

13

MICHELLE   I came out of the bathroom and we started talking.

ARTHUR   Talking? He could barely get a word out when I was in there.

MICHELLE   Well he was really talking up a storm with me.

ARTHUR   Go on.

MICHELLE   So then he asked me to sit down and I started to bring the chair over, but he said no and patted the bed.

NORMAN   Hello.

MICHELLE   So I sat down on the bed and we were talking . . .

ARTHUR   About what?

MICHELLE   Baseball. He asked me how I thought the Orioles would do this year.

ARTHUR   Don't you think it's odd that he's still interested in baseball?

NORMAN (*quickly dismissing*)   Yeah, yeah, it's odd. It's very odd. So then what happened?

MICHELLE   Okay . . . So then as he was talking, all of a sudden he reached over and put his hand on my boob.

NORMAN   Unbelievable.

ARTHUR   You think you know someone.

NORMAN   And what did you do?

MICHELLE   Well he has one or two days, if not a few hours, to live. What's the big deal? So he put his hand on my boob. Who cares?

NORMAN   What a fantastic attitude! Sure, it's just a hand. What's a hand? People put their hands on my shoulder. I'm aware of the hand. "Hey, there's a hand on my shoulder." But it's not so terrible. Eventually they take it off.

MICHELLE Right.

NORMAN Hey, let me ask you this. Do you think he knew what he was doing or is it possible the hand just kind of landed there?

MICHELLE Oh he knew what he was doing.

ARTHUR Why do you say that?

MICHELLE Because he squeezed it.

NORMAN What kind of squeeze?

MICHELLE A normal breast squeeze.

NORMAN Like two seconds?

MICHELLE Mmm . . . Yeah, that sounds right.

NORMAN How many squeezes were there?

MICHELLE Quite a few.

NORMAN What kind of pressure was applied?

MICHELLE Medium to hard.

ARTHUR So how long, all tolled, was his hand on there?

MICHELLE Hard to say. I lost track of time.

ARTHUR So eventually he took it off?

MICHELLE Yes, but then he put it someplace else.

ARTHUR And where was that?

MICHELLE My leg.

ARTHUR He put his hand on your leg?

MICHELLE With no compunction.

NORMAN And was the hand active in any way or was it just sort of resting there for the most part?

MICHELLE Oh, there was activity.

15

NORMAN   He inched up?

MICHELLE   He inched up. But then, much to my surprise, he removed his hand and put it back on my boob.

NORMAN   Interesting, inasmuch as he was making progress *there*, he chose to retreat to *there*.

MICHELLE   Anyway, that's when your mother came in.

ARTHUR   It's remarkable. It never ends. A man's dying and this is what he's thinking about.

MICHELLE   I thought we were just exchanging pleasantries.

ARTHUR (*to Michelle*)   I think you should probably go home. I'll give you a call. My mother's going to be coming out of there any second and it's going to be really awkward.

MICHELLE   Would you please tell her why I did it?

ARTHUR   Yeah, I'm sure she'll be very understanding.

MICHELLE   Bye, bye, Norman.

NORMAN   Bye . . . A pleasure to meet you.

MICHELLE   Thank you . . . And I'm so sorry.

   She leaves.

NORMAN   Oh my God, that Michelle character . . . (*in reverence*) Get outta town . . .

ARTHUR   Tell me about it.

NORMAN   You tell *me* about it!

ARTHUR   Well, the sex is out of control, but other than that, I have nothing to say to her.

NORMAN   So what do you do when you're not having sex?

ARTHUR   We don't do anything but go out to dinner, and I eat fast. Really fast . . . You know what else? She likes women too.

16

NORMAN No.

ARTHUR Yes.

NORMAN Please tell me you're joking.

ARTHUR I'm not.

NORMAN And have you . . .

ARTHUR Not yet, but it's on the table.

NORMAN That's so unfair. Have you ever been with two women?

ARTHUR Oh yeah. I assume you haven't?

NORMAN Well . . . I once sat between two women in coach.

*The elevator doors open and FABIANA, the Puerto Rican
housekeeper, early 40s, steps off. She's taking this very hard.*

FABIANA (*to Norman*) Hello, Mr. Drexel.

ARTHUR Hey, Fabiana.

NORMAN Hey, Fabiana. So nice of you to come.

FABIANA Of course . . . Can I go in to see your father?

NORMAN Yes, but he's not very alert. It's not looking good.

*Fabiana starts to break down and mumbles something in Spanish.
Norman awkwardly pats her arm. As she takes a step toward
Sidney's room:*

You know, Fabiana, I meant to tell you. I keep forgetting . . .

Fabiana turns back.

I don't think the dishwasher is getting the silverware clean. I think
you need to rinse off the knives and forks before you put them in.
Or maybe just wash them separately, 'cause it's kind of gross.

FABIANA (*through tears*) Then why bother with the dishwasher?
It's like washing your hands before you shower.

NORMAN   Very good point, Fabiana. I must say, I'm no fan of the dishwasher. I prefer to do it by hand. I have much more confidence in a hand wash.

FABIANA   Well if you want me to rinse them off, I can rinse them off.

NORMAN   Just something to keep in the back of your head.

FABIANA   Okay.

Gloria emerges from Sidney's room, passes Fabiana, and gives her a funny look.

GLORIA   Oh . . . Fabiana.

FABIANA (*curtly*)   Hello.

Fabiana continues into Sidney's room.

GLORIA   What the hell is your maid doing here?

NORMAN   What are you talking about? She worked for you and Dad for ten years.

GLORIA   And she was terrible!

NORMAN   Oh yeah, like you're a day at the beach!

Now Brenda reenters with her daughter, NATALIE, early 20s. She's with her goofy boyfriend, GREG.

BRENDA   Look who I found.

NATALIE (*with proper British accent*)   Hello, Uncle Arthur.

They hug. Arthur gives Norman a look.

NORMAN   Hello! Well if it isn't Miss Doolittle herself.

NATALIE   Hello, Father.

They also hug.

GLORIA   I don't get a hello?

NATALIE Forgive me, Grandmother. Terribly sorry. Nasty business.

They, too, hug.

GLORIA Why are you talking like that?

BRENDA She's in character.

NATALIE I'm playing Liza Doolittle.

GLORIA Eliza Doolittle has a cockney accent. She's not proper.

GREG Well she is after Professor Higgins gets through with her.

NATALIE (*cockney*) I 'ave to do both.

NORMAN (*to Natalie*) Do you really need to be doing that here?

NATALIE (*back to proper, employed for the remainder of the act*) Don't be cross, Father.

To Gloria.

Grandmother, you remember my boyfriend, Greg?

GREG Hi. I am so sorry for your loss.

GLORIA He's not dead yet.

We hear a wail from Fabiana in Sidney's room.

BRENDA (*to Norman*) Fabiana?

NORMAN She's visiting.

GREG Could it smell any worse in here?

GLORIA He's shy, isn't he?

NATALIE But it is unpleasant.

GREG Unpleasant's an understatement . . . Let me ask you. Can you die from an odor?

NORMAN Not a terrible question.

GREG   I mean, if something really stunk and you had to smell it all the time?

NATALIE   If you could, I'd already be dead.

GREG   Norman, how funny is she?

Dr. Stiles enters. Another wail from Fabiana.

DR. STILES   What's that?

NORMAN   Our housekeeper. She used to work for my dad.

DR. STILES   Any news on the ventilator?

NORMAN   Yeah . . . We're not doing it.

DR. STILES   Good decision.

He exits. Norman and Greg find themselves paired up.

GREG   Was that your dad's doctor?

NORMAN   Yeah.

GREG   Did you tip him? (*he places his hand on Norman's shoulder*)

NORMAN   Tip him?

GREG   Sure, you should give him something.

NORMAN   Really? (*Norman swats at Greg's arm, which removes the hand*)

GREG   Positively.

NORMAN   I never heard of that.

GREG (*putting his hand back on Norman's shoulder*)   Oh, it's appropriate. My dad does it all the time.

NORMAN   Hmm. How much? (*he swats Greg's hand away again*)

GREG   One or two hundred at the very least.

Fabiana wails again. Then the elevator doors open and an older couple step out. They are Sidney's sister, ROSE, and her husband HARRY.

Pudgy Rose has been the happiest of women since the day she married her shifty husband. Everyone adlibs their hellos to them.

ARTHUR   Hi, Aunt Rose.

HARRY   Brenda, Norman, Arthur . . .

ROSE   I'm so sorry, Gloria.

GLORIA *(looks at her watch)*   Oh, you finally decided to come?

HARRY   How is he?

NORMAN   Not great.

HARRY   Okay if we go in?

NORMAN   Sure, but there's someone in there.

HARRY *(to Norman)*   So how's the lawyer?

NORMAN   That's Arthur.

ROSE *(re: Norman)*   He makes toilets, Harry. You know that.

NORMAN   They're not toilets, they're urinals. There's a difference.

HARRY   They wish they were toilets.

Fabiana exits Sidney's room.

ROSE   Oh, it's the cleaning lady! Hello!

A distraught Fabiana ignores her, along with everyone else, and continues to the elevators.

She's awfully rude.

NORMAN   Well, she's upset. She worked for my father a long time.

ROSE   Big deal. I'm his sister. You say hello.

HARRY   You can nod, for crissakes!

ROSE   That's all I'm asking for, Norman. A simple nod. You move your head.

Sidney's blustery, bull-in-a-china-shop, younger brother, STEWIE, steps out of the elevator. He's never had a conversation that someone didn't overhear.

STEWIE   You live a virtuous life and for what?!

NORMAN (*gestures for him to keep it down*)   Inside voice, Uncle Stew.

STEWIE   I am inside.

NORMAN   It's a little raucous for a hospital.

STEWIE   Hello, Gloria.

He kisses her.

GLORIA   Stewart.

STEWIE   Rose . . . Harry. Hello, Natalie.

NATALIE   Uncle Stewart.

STEWIE (*to Norman*)   How is he? Can I go see him?

HARRY   Well we were just about to go in.

STEWIE   We can all go in together.

HARRY   Actually, if you don't mind, we'd like to go in by ourselves.

STEWIE   "If I don't mind?" Why can't we all go in together?

ROSE   Look, we'll just be a minute.

STEWIE   Nothing takes a minute.

HARRY   Two at the most.

STEWIE   Now it's already up to two.

ROSE   I want to say good-bye to him and it's personal.

STEWIE You weren't even close to him!

ROSE He was best man at my wedding!

STEWIE That's 'cause he's got no friends!

HARRY I've got friends!

STEWIE They're all in prison.

GLORIA Stewart, let them go in!

STEWIE Ahh, go ahead! (*he waves them off*)

ROSE (*snidely*) Thank you.

They go in.

STEWIE He's a real pleasure, that Harry. Top prick . . . So, Gloria, what's new?

GLORIA What's new? My husband's dying.

NORMAN Maybe not such a good question.

Gloria exits.

GREG (*to Brenda*) April 19, 2007.

NORMAN Oh, God.

BRENDA . . . Oh, that's a special one. It was a rainy Thursday. I did the crossword puzzle, missed 51 Across. *Quarterback who led the Jets to victory at Super Bowl III* . . . Namath. Then Sidney came over and gave us that hideous portrait he painted of Gloria. And with Norman's permission, he hung it right in the living room. I've had to look at that monstrosity for the last seven years.

NORMAN It was a gift.

BRENDA So what? Your mother gave me a grotesque, woolen, argyle scarf for my birthday one year. I don't wear it. It's not a big deal.

STEWIE (*re: Harry and Rose*)   What are they doing in there? (*getting worked up*) What if something happens and I don't get to see him?

ARTHUR   Nothing's going to happen.

STEWIE   I betcha Harry'll stay longer on purpose just to piss me off!

NORMAN   He's not going to doing that.

STEWIE   You don't know him, Norman. He is!

NORMAN   No, he's not!

STEWIE   He thinks I'm going to stand for this bullshit? I don't stand for bullshit, Norman! (*he starts for Sidney's room*)

NORMAN   Stewie, don't go in there.

Stewie continues for the door.

Stewie!

But Stewie will not be deterred and barges in.

STEWIE (*O.S.*)   It's not going to work!

HARRY (*O.S.*)   Will you get the hell out of here?

STEWIE (*O.S.*)   No, time's up. You get out!

ROSE (*O.S.*)   Get out, Stew! What's wrong with you?

STEWIE (*O.S.*)   Who do you think you are?

ROSE (*O.S.*)   You're a lunatic!

HARRY (*O.S. panicked*)   Sidney! Sidney!

HARRY/STEWIE (*O.S.*)   Sidney!

HARRY/STEWIE/ROSE (*O.S.*)   Sidney!

(*Rose, Harry, and Stewie rush out*)

ARTHUR   What's going on?

STEWIE   Something happened!

NORMAN   What happened?

HARRY   Someone get the doctor!

STEWIE   Who? Who should get the doctor?

HARRY   I don't know! Somebody!

STEWIE   Okay, so you go!

HARRY   No, you go!

STEWIE   Rose, get a doctor!

ROSE   You go!

BRENDA   Oh for God's sake! I'll go.

Brenda waves them off and marches out to find the doctor.

STEWIE   That's okay, I'll go.

HARRY   No, I'll go.

STEWIE   Oh, 'cause I said I was going? Now you wanna go?

Blackout

Stage lights up on Sidney's room, where everyone, including Dr. Stiles, has gathered around the bed of the once mighty Sidney Drexel. The end is nigh.

NORMAN Dad . . . Dad . . .

NATALIE Quiet, he's trying to say something.

SIDNEY I love you, Gloria.

GLORIA What?

NORMAN He said he loves you.

GLORIA I love you, too, Sidney.

SIDNEY I love you, Norm-al.

NORMAN	**ARTHUR**
I love you too, Dad.	I love you too, Dad.

ARTHUR He was talking to me. He said I love you, Toro. He calls me Toro.

NORMAN He said Norm-al. He calls me Normal.

SIDNEY Who's that? Stewie?

STEWIE Yes, Sidney.

ROSE And your sister, Rose.

HARRY I'm here too.

SIDNEY Who's that?

HARRY Harry.

SIDNEY Harry Gold?

HARRY Harry Kanter, your brother-in-law.

SIDNEY Oh.

SIDNEY (*glancing toward Norman and Arthur*) Listen, I want you to do something for me.

26

ARTHUR	**NORMAN**
Of course.	You name it.

ARTHUR   He was talking to me.

NORMAN   He was talking to me.

SIDNEY   I want you to always take care of your mother.

ARTHUR	**NORMAN**
Absolutely!	Yes, of course, of course!

SIDNEY   I don't want her to live alone.

NORMAN	**ARTHUR**
What?	What?

SIDNEY   I want her to come live with you.

NORMAN   Me?

ARHTUR   Me?

SIDNEY   Exactly.

NORMAN	**ARTHUR**
(*pointing to Arthur*)	(*pointing to Norman*)
Who? Him?	Who? Him?

SIDNEY   Promise me. Promise me you won't let her live alone in that big house.

Long silence . . .

NORMAN   Promise him.

ARTHUR   He was talking to you.

NORMAN   He was talking to you.

GLORIA   Sidney, who were you talking to? Sidney?

NORMAN   Dad?! Dad!

NATALIE   Grandpa.

GREG   Mr. Drexel.

BRENDA   Sidney.

GLORIA   Oh my God.

ARTHUR   Dad, who were you talking to?

NORMAN   Dad, who were you talking to! Who the hell were you talking to?!

Dr. Stiles checks Sidney's stats then shakes his head.

Blackout

Sidney's hospital room, a few minutes later. Except for Natalie and Greg, all Principals are present, including the dead body.

ARTHUR   Oh come on. He was looking right at you.

NORMAN   No way. He was looking at you. How much you want to bet?

ARTHUR   I'll bet you whatever you want. A thousand!

NORMAN   Ten thousand!

ARTHUR   Ten thousand? You don't even have ten thousand!

NORMAN   I can get ten thousand!

ARTHUR   You can get ten thousand?!

BRENDA   Will the two of you stop it? Your father's been dead for five minutes. What's the matter with you? You should be ashamed of yourselves! Anyway, it's all so ridiculous . . .

To Arthur.

He was looking right at you.

ARTHUR (*to the Nurse and Dr. Stiles*)   Doctor, could we talk to you both for a second? You were here. Were you able to tell who he was talking to?

NURSE (*to Arthur*)   First I thought he was talking to you and then he seemed to switch.

NORMAN (*to Nurse*)   How dare you.

ARTHUR (*to Norman*)   Okay?

DR. STILES   That's not the way I saw it. He started with you and then ended up with you.

Norman reacts in kind.

ARTHUR   Thank you. That's very helpful . . .

29

Gloria begins to cry.

DR. STILES The mortician should be here soon . . . I'm sorry for your loss.

GLORIA Thank you.

Dr. Stiles and the Nurse head for the door.

ARTHUR Let's wait outside. This is morbid.

To Dr. Stiles.

How long does it usually take for them to get here?

DR. STILES Not sure. Could be fifteen minutes. Could be two hours.

ROSE You'd think as soon as somebody dies, they'd get swooped up.

STEWIE She's right. You can't just leave the guy lying here. It's like at a restaurant after a meal—the busboy clears away the plates . . . He needs to be bussed.

DR. STILES On that note . . .

Dr. Stiles and the Nurse leave. Norman remembers something and follows them out.

Lights down on Sidney's room. Lights up on the lounge.

NORMAN Hey, Doc.

He reaches into his pocket and removes a wad of bills.

Just wanted to thank you for everything. Here's a small token of my appreciation . . . Use it in good health. Go buy yourself a new stethoscope.

DR. STILES What are you doing? You're giving me a tip?

NORMAN Yeah.

DR. STILES Seriously?

NORMAN   I thought it was customary.

DR. STILES   I assure you it is not customary. That's the first one I've ever been offered.

NORMAN   Is that so?

DR. STILES   Yes, that's so.

NORMAN (*turning to the Nurse*)   Have you ever heard of tipping a doctor?

The Nurse laughs.

That's what I thought. I think I've just been had.

NURSE   Well now you have the fun of getting even.

NORMAN   So I do, Nurse Ramirez. So I shall.

SR, we pick up on a conversation already underway.

HARRY (*forcefully to Stewie*)   I was talking to him. We were having a nice conversation. Then you barged in, started screaming, and he died. You killed him!

STEWIE   He was about to die any minute.

ROSE   Any minute? What are you, a doctor?

STEWIE   I'm sorry. It came from a good place.

HARRY   Where's that?

STEWIE (*defensive*)   Fine. I'm leaving.

ROSE   Oh that's right! As soon as things get a little sticky, the tough guy leaves.

STEWIE   What do you want me to do, sleep here?

ARTHUR   All right, enough. Give us a break.

STEWIE   . . . Gloria, I'm sorry. Did I kill him?

GLORIA   You didn't help.

STEWIE So this is how it's going to be? The only reason I was even civil to you people was out of respect for my brother. Now that he's gone, we're done. (*Stewie starts to leave, then stops abruptly*) If you don't mind . . . I'll just be a minute. (*he enters the bathroom and shuts the door*)

HARRY Well, Rose, we should also get going.

ROSE Yes we should.

They say their good-byes. On their way out, Harry stops by the bed and addresses Sidney's corpse.

HARRY Good-bye, Sidney. You were one of my favorite people. And it was so nice of you to promise me your Rolex. I'll wear it every day and think of you. What a beautiful parting gift. I'll cherish it for the rest of my life. Thank you, Sidney. Take care.

GLORIA Sidney said you could have his Rolex?

HARRY Yes . . . wasn't that a beautiful gesture?

GLORIA When did he say that?

HARRY Earlier when I was in the room talking to him.

GLORIA Doesn't sound like Sidney.

ROSE That's what he said, Gloria.

HARRY I even said to him, "Are you sure, Sidney? Is that what you want to do?" He said, "Harry, I've never been more certain of anything in my life."

NORMAN No kidding.

HARRY You don't have to give it to me right away. I'll pick it up.

As he and Rose start to exit—

NORMAN Take care of those big balls.

They leave. As soon as they're out the door:

32

GLORIA What a liar. A filthy liar.

ARTHUR That really takes the cake.

BRENDA Wow.

GLORIA He'll get that watch over my dead body.

NORMAN Actually, Dad promised that watch to me.

ARTHUR He did? When?

NORMAN You think I'm making that up? He told me that watch was mine.

ARTHUR You couldn't wear that watch anyway! You're not a Rolex guy.

NORMAN Oh, you are? You are?!

ARTHUR I'm more Rolex than you!

NORMAN I'm much more Rolex than you! Ma, who's more Rolex?

GLORIA Oh, for God's sake.

To Brenda.

Where did Natalie go?

BRENDA She left with Greg. He had to go to work.

NORMAN Oh! She's got my credit card. (*he runs out*)

GLORIA She's taking this acting thing too far. Who goes around talking like that?

BRENDA Well, she's finally found something to focus on. And she's in a very serious relationship with Greg, who I happen to like a lot.

GLORIA He's not the brightest bulb in the box, that one. I think he's got ADHD.

BRENDA   He's actually trying to become a life coach.

GLORIA   I rest my case.

BRENDA   Well I think it's pretty impressive.

ARTHUR   It's great that you like him. My father didn't care for my ex.

BRENDA (*half-joking*)   Or me.

ARTHUR (*laughing*)   Well that's true.

BRENDA (*this comes as bit of a surprise for Brenda*)   What?

ARTHUR   The day you guys got married, my dad told Norman he didn't have to go through with it.

BRENDA   Excuse me?

ARTHUR   Norman never told you? Oh, well . . . um, he thought you were . . . too young.

BRENDA (*skeptical*)   Too young?

ARTHUR   Mom, will you tell her? Wasn't that it?

GLORIA   Well I'm not gonna lie. He never liked you.

BRENDA   What did I ever do to him?

Norman enters and catches that.

NORMAN   What's going on?

BRENDA   Your mother was just about to tell me why your father didn't like me.

NORMAN   What? Oh come on. Why is it that after someone dies all of a sudden people decide to become honest? Not only is honesty not the best policy, it's actually the worst of all possible policies.

BRENDA   No, I want to hear this.

GLORIA You wanna hear? Okay. Twelve years ago, you invited us for dinner. You served fish. You dimmed the lights and it was so dark in that dining room, you couldn't see the bones. Sidney almost choked to death. I remember twice he asked you to turn up the dimmer and you know what you said? You know what you said?

BRENDA I know exactly what I said, but why don't you refresh my memory.

GLORIA Tell her, Arthur.

ARTHUR You said, "This is my house."

BRENDA I like to dim the lights a little when I eat. Your house is like a Baskin-Robbins.

GLORIA Who eats fish in the dark? It's insane. Poor Sidney was retching for half an hour. I thought we were going to have to take him to the hospital.

NORMAN It was twelve years ago!

GLORIA He never forgot it and neither did I! Fish in the dark!

NORMAN It wasn't even that dark!

ARTHUR I couldn't see it.

NORMAN I had no problem.

BRENDA Me neither.

GLORIA You were near the kitchen. You had more light.

NORMAN So he swallowed a bone and that was it?

GLORIA And what about that beautiful scarf we gave her for her birthday years ago and she never wore it? Not once! Not once! I've seen her in a hundred different scarves since then. She bought scarves on purpose just to annoy us.

BRENDA I don't wear wool. It itches.

35

GLORIA   It itches? Oh, I'm sorry your neck is so delicate.

NORMAN (*to Gloria*)   Will you stop it?!

Brenda gathers her things. She's heard enough.

GLORIA   You're so scared of her! She snaps her fingers and you jump. She doesn't appreciate you and she never did from day one!

BRENDA   You know what? I look forward to getting that middle-of-the-night call about visiting you right here. The sooner, the better.

NORMAN (*to Brenda*)   Oh, come on.

Brenda leaves, just as the MORTICIANS enter. Norman gestures to the bed.

Right there.

GLORIA   Oh my God.

As the Morticians put Sidney on the gurney and wheel him out, we hear a toilet flush. Stewie opens the bathroom door. Everyone turns and stares.

STEWIE   What?

Blackout

SCENE 5

Lights up on Gloria's dining room. CS, a long table with a spread of food and pastries. Behind it is a smaller, rectangular table, which serves as a makeshift bar. There are a few dining room chairs scattered about.

UL are French doors, which lead to the patio, where most of the family will gather.

A door, SR, leads to the street. Norman and Brenda, wearing funeral garb, enter through the French doors.

BRENDA How you holding up?

NORMAN Okay.

BRENDA You know, Norman, you don't have to pretend. At the funeral, I saw you covering your face and shaking.

NORMAN No . . . I was trying not to vomit from an acid reflux attack.

BRENDA Ohhh . . . that's what that was.

NORMAN Yeah, it was a bad one.

BRENDA So besides the Louis XIV decor, this isn't a bad house. I don't see why we can't just get her a dog for company.

NORMAN She hates all animals. She looks at extinction as a good thing.

BRENDA Well then you need to talk to Arthur soon because I'll move out before she moves in with us. Could you imagine?

NORMAN Oh, we'd kill each other.

BRENDA I think I'd kill you first so your mother would suffer more.

NORMAN If you ever killed me, she'd drown you in the toilet bowl, then impale you and use your head for a tchotchke.

37

Brenda takes a piece of food from Norman's plate.

What are you doing? There's a whole table full of food.

Now the other Drexels and their Family and Friends begin to straggle in, also wearing funeral garb.

ARTHUR   I could use a drink.

To Stewie.

Do you want something?

STEWIE   Now you're talking!

ARTHUR   Mom, where do you keep the liquor?

GLORIA   It's right in front of your face.

NORMAN (*to Arthur, trying to sound casual*)   So you didn't invite Michelle to the funeral . . . ?

ARTHUR   I'm not seeing her anymore. Didn't want to touch her after Dad copped a feel. Eeech . . .

STEWIE   I gotta tell ya, Norm, the only time I feel truly alive is at funerals. It's like life is an elimination tournament and I've moved on to the next round.

NORMAN   Very touching, Stewie. I should've mentioned that in my eulogy.

STEWIE   You gave a good eulogy, Norm, but you finished a distant second.

NORMAN   Yes, Jessica was very good.

STEWIE   Good? Great. Arthur must be very proud.

A beat, as everyone settles. Gloria sighs.

GLORIA   I never would have believed it. Sidney's gone.

BRENDA   One down, one to go.

GLORIA   They should have eulogies when people are alive so at least they can hear it.

ARTHUR   Good point, Mom.

GLORIA (*to Norman*)   All I know is I hope you say such nice things about me at my funeral.

NORMAN   Nicer!

GLORIA   Really? There's something nice to say?

NORMAN (*fumbling*)   Uh . . . Sure, sure. Yeah, yeah . . . Sure. I'll come up with something.

JAY LEVENTHAL, mid-50s, approaches Norman and Arthur.

JAY (*to Arthur*)   So I hear you're dating my notary, Michelle.

ARTHUR   I was.

NORMAN   She's something.

JAY   That she is . . . Your dad was quite a guy. I wish I'd known he was in the hospital. Most of my clients are senior citizens. I'm over there more than I'm at my office.

ARTHUR   He always liked you, Jay.

JAY   Boy, he gave me a lot of good laughs.

NORMAN   He was the funniest.

To Stewie.

This is Jay Leventhal, my dad's lawyer and estate planner. This is my Uncle Stewie.

STEWIE   Nice to meet you. If I ever get an estate, I'll give you a call.

To Norman.

I'm funnier than your father!

39

NATALIE (*employing proper voice for the entire scene*) With all due respect, dear Uncle, I beg to disagree. There was nary a man who could match wits with darling Sidney.

STEWIE Where is this play you're doing? I want to come see it.

NATALIE It's in a work space above the Hooters on Cahuenga Boulevard. Shall I put you down for two?

STEWIE I'll tell you later.

Rose and Harry enter and head straight for Gloria.

ROSE Gloria, it was a lovely service.

HARRY I was crying like a baby.

GLORIA Forget it, Harry. You're not getting the Rolex.

HARRY But Sidney said—

GLORIA Please, Harry. Sidney said? I know Sidney . . . His last words were not going to be, "Harry, you can have my Rolex." He'd rather die.

HARRY Gloria, as God as my witness.

GLORIA I don't care if Lindbergh's maid was your witness. You're not getting it . . .

ROSE Come on, Harry. I've heard enough.

To Gloria.

You've got some nerve.

GLORIA I've got a nerve?

As Rose and Harry head to the door, Rose can't resist stopping at the buffet table.

ROSE (*to Harry*) You want a sandwich?

HARRY What do they have?

ROSE Tuna, pastrami, egg salad . . .

HARRY Egg salad? It'll stink up the car.

NORMAN Just pick one!

Rose and Harry leave with the sandwiches, as more Family and Friends arrive, among them, Arthur's fourteen-year-old daughter, JESSICA.

ARTHUR Oh there she is! My daughter, ladies and gentlemen. How fantastic was she?

Very, according to the assemblage.

GLORIA Come here, sweetheart. I want to give you a hug.

Jessica gets the full treatment.

You were so wonderful. I'm so proud of you. Grandpa would be too.

JESSICA Thank you, Grandma.

GLORIA You had the best speech. Better than Norman. Norman, she was better than you.

NORMAN Yes, yes. She was very good.

GLORIA Fourteen years old.

To Norman.

Could you write a beautiful eulogy like that when you were fourteen?

NORMAN No, I could not.

ARTHUR Yeah, well, she worked very hard on it. How 'bout this kid?!

NORMAN (*finds Brenda*) You listening to this bullshit?

BRENDA Hard not to.

41

NORMAN   I don't think she wrote a word of that.

BRENDA   You don't, do you?

NORMAN   No, I don't.

BRENDA (*mocking*)   Oh, so Arthur did?

NORMAN   Uh, yeah!

BRENDA   Because he wanted to show you up.

NORMAN   There you go.

BRENDA   I think you're nuts.

NORMAN   Are you kidding? No fourteen-year-old could write like that. She used the word "profound." No way she knows that word.

BRENDA   Profound? What's the big whoop with profound?

NORMAN   Big whoop? Since when do you say "whoop"?

BRENDA   I say whoop.

NORMAN   I've never heard you say whoop.

BRENDA   Anyway, you'll never know.

NORMAN   That's what you think.

BRENDA   No. Don't.

NORMAN   It'll be very easy.

BRENDA   Everyone will just think you're jealous because, the truth is, she was better.

NORMAN   *Et tu, Brendus?*

BRENDA   Don't you have more important things to do, like talk to Arthur? I'm not kidding, Norman. This is not just a painting. She's alive. In the flesh. It's time to walk the talk.

NORMAN   You mean talk the talk.

BRENDA   No, you're walking over there, so it's walk the talk.

NORMAN   Look, you either talk the talk or walk the walk! You can't mix up the walking and the talking!

BRENDA   Well you don't know what you're walking or talking about!

She heads off, leaving Norman alone. A few beats later, Jessica enters. Norman brightens. He gives her the once-over, then:

NORMAN   Hey.

JESSICA   Hi.

NORMAN   So that was a wonderful, wonderful eulogy.

JESSICA   Thank you, Uncle Norman.

NORMAN   And you used the word "profound." That's a big word.

JESSICA   It's not so big.

NORMAN   Oh it's kind of big. Profound. That's a real grown-up word. Where'd you come across that one?

GLORIA *(screams)*   Sidney! Sidney!

All eyes turn to Gloria.

Sidney was here!

ARTHUR   Mom, calm down. What are you talking about?

GLORIA   The bird out there. You didn't see it? It was right there.

ARTHUR   So what?

GLORIA   It was an Oriole. Daddy was from Baltimore. He was an Oriole fan. That was a sign from Sidney! He said he was going to give me a sign and that was it!

NORMAN   Mom, are you crazy? They'll put you in the nut house . . . It was just a bird.

43

GLORIA It wasn't a bird. It was Sidney.

NORMAN So I don't understand. What if it was Dad? Is that a good thing? Dad's a bird?

GLORIA Sidney!

As she runs outside to the Garden Patio area, everyone follows except Norman and Greg.

NORMAN Dad's a bird! It's a bird, it's a plane, it's Sidney! . . . What a freak show!

GREG Hey, Norman?

NORMAN Oh, hey, Greg.

GREG Could I talk to you for a second?

NORMAN Sure.

GREG (*with some difficulty*) So Natalie and I have been together for over a year now and . . . well . . . Norman I'd really like to marry her. Of course, I wouldn't ask her without your blessing first . . .

NORMAN (*putting him on*) My blessing . . . My blessing . . . Hmm . . . You know what? I-I-I-I . . . don't think so. Nope. Not feeling it, Greggy boy.

GREG You're denying the blessing?

NORMAN Yeah . . . not blessing-inclined right now. Too soon. Maybe a couple years. Sorry.

Arthur reenters. Greg exits.

ARTHUR Thanks for all your help. That was really pleasant . . . I was just thinking how out of control Mom's going to be now. Dad was the only one she listened to. She worshipped the guy.

NORMAN I know . . . So look, we need to discuss this living situation with Mom.

ARTHUR Why can't she just live here?

NORMAN Because her husband died and she doesn't want to.

ARTHUR So she has to live with one of us?

NORMAN It was Dad's dying wish. And he asked you. You know that.

ARTHUR Oh come on. He was looking at you.

NORMAN No. He was looking at you.

ARTHUR Even the nurse said so.

NORMAN The doctor said he was looking at you. Who would know more, a doctor or a nurse?

ARTHUR A nurse. They're always more attuned to the patient.

NORMAN I've had bad nurses. They can be very gruff.

ARTHUR Well she can't live with me, so that's out of the question.

NORMAN Listen, I would do it, even though I don't want to, but Brenda has already told me she'll leave me. She hates her. Mom cannot stay with us.

ARTHUR Look, Norman, I swear I'd do it if Dad asked me or Mom asked me.

NORMAN Hey, I've got an idea. Well Dad's dead, and he did ask you. And Mom wouldn't ask you that in a million years . . . Hey, I got it. She rotates!

ARTHUR Rotates? You mean going from house to house like kids whose parents are divorced? No, Norman, I won't do that. She needs a safe and secure environment . . . Your house.

NORMAN Don't you understand?! I just explained. I can't! Brenda will leave me.

ARTHUR Blessing in Disguise. It will change your life. You'll thank me.

NORMAN So that's it? You're not going to take her?

ARTHUR Nope. You need to learn to say no, Norman. It's very liberating.

NORMAN Yes, I suppose it frees you up to be a thoughtless douchebag.

Arthur rejoins everyone outside. Norman begins to pace. He's interrupted by Fabiana.

FABIANA Hello, Mr. Drexel.

NORMAN Hey, Fabiana. Oh, look you brought a little something.

FABIANA Some cuchi fritos.

NORMAN Oh, cuchi fritos . . . I didn't know you were coming.

FABIANA Well I work for your father a long time.

NORMAN Yes, until I stole you.

FABIANA You no steal me, Mr. Drexel. I quit . . . Mr. Drexel . . . (*she closes the door*)

NORMAN Again with the door . . .

FABIANA . . . I need to talk to you about something.

NORMAN Sure.

FABIANA This is not easy to say . . .

NORMAN Okay . . . Go ahead.

FABIANA It was twenty years ago. I had been working for your parents maybe eight months. One day I was in the laundry room and Mr. Sidney came up behind me and grabbed my *tetas* and started rubbing up against me.

NORMAN What? My father grabbed your *tetas*?!

FABIANA   *Sí.* Your father. This is true.

Jay enters.

Hello.

Offering one.

Cuchi frito?

JAY   Jay Leventhal. (*he takes it and exits*)

NORMAN   Oh God . . . Go on.

FABIANA   Anyway, I couldn't stop him, but Mr. Drexel, I didn't want to stop him. We wound up having *chingando* right there in the laundry room.

NORMAN   *Chingando?* With my father? In the laundry room?

FABIANA   He said it was the safest room in the house, that your mother would never set foot in there.

NORMAN   And it was just that . . . one time?

FABIANA   No. I worked there three days a week, so we did it six times a week . . . That's an average.

NORMAN   That's an average?

FABIANA   Well, sometimes we'd only do it once or twice. Other times we'd do it ten, twelve, fourteen—

NORMAN   Fourteen?! I thought he was tired from work . . . So did he ever see you outside the house?

FABIANA   Oh yes. He would take me out to restaurants. And once we went to a dude ranch.

NORMAN   My father took you to a dude ranch?

FABIANA   Yes.

A SERVER enters from SL, and places a plate on the food table. Norman and Fabiana immediately shift the conversation.

NORMAN   I love horses.

FABIANA   Me too.

NORMAN   Beautiful creatures.

FABIANA   I do sidesaddle.

NORMAN   I do bareback.

Once the Server is gone, Fabiana and Norman resume their actual conversation.

NORMAN   . . . Wow, all this time I thought you quit because of my mother.

FABIANA   No. The truth is I left because of Diego.

NORMAN   Diego? Your son? What did he have to do with anything?

Fabiana gives him a long look, raising her eyebrows. A few beats, then:

Oh no . . . No, no . . . No, no, no!

FABIANA   Yes, yes, yes.

NORMAN   No . . . No . . . That's not good. Fabiana, it's not good . . . It's not good!

FABIANA   When Diego got older, he started to look so much like your father that I couldn't bring him to the house. Anyway, Sidney told me he'd always take care of us. He said he was going to speak to you about me.

NORMAN   Me?

FABIANA   Yes, you . . . Or maybe it was your brother.

NORMAN   Yes, Arthur! It was Arthur!

FABIANA   I'm not sure. It was the last time I saw him, when he was in the hospital. He said a name I never hear before.

NORMAN Was it Toro? Normal?

FABIANA One of those two.

NORMAN Of course it was Arthur. He has way more money than me. Why would my father want you to talk to me?

FABIANA I don't know.

NORMAN Fabiana, does anyone else know about this?

FABIANA No, no one.

NORMAN Listen, would you do me a favor?

FABIANA If it's not a big one.

NORMAN Would you tell Arthur that my father wanted him to take care of Diego?

FABIANA I'm sorry, Mr. Drexel. I can't. I don't know him like that. But someone has to take care of us. Diego wants to go to college and it's expensive.

NORMAN College? Really?

FABIANA Yes.

NORMAN You know, I went to college. It's a complete waste of time.

FABIANA Not for my Diego. He will learn. He's a good boy.

NORMAN Of course he is.

FABIANA And then he wants to go to medical school.

NORMAN Why wouldn't he? I would imagine he might want to study abroad, as well.

FABIANA No, but that sounds like a very good idea. I will mention it to him.

NORMAN Look, Fabiana, can I be honest with you? I can't afford all this. The urinal business has not been great.

FABIANA (*getting emotional*)   So what are you saying? You are not going to help us? What's wrong with you? This is your brother . . . This is your blood.

NORMAN   All right, we'll work it out.

FABIANA   You promise?

NORMAN   Close to promising . . . Eighty-five percent promise . . . Ninety-six percent promise . . .

Fabiana leaves. Norman frantically motions to Arthur to come back inside.

Close the doors, close the doors.

Arthur does.

So guess what?

ARTHUR   I give up.

NORMAN   Ready for this?

ARTHUR   Yeah, I'm ready.

NORMAN   . . . We have a brother.

ARTHUR   We have a brother? What are you talking about?

NORMAN   Fabiana's son, Diego . . . Dad's his father.

ARTHUR   What?!

NORMAN   Yup.

ARTHUR   Are you fucking kidding me?

NORMAN   Nope.

ARTHUR   I swear, the last time I saw that kid he was twelve and I thought, "There's something about him that looks familiar." But I couldn't figure it out.

NORMAN   Can you believe Dad? I thought that breast thing in the hospital was an aberration, but apparently it's the tip of the iceberg.

ARTHUR   I can see it. To be perfectly honest, I've had the same thought about Fabiana.

NORMAN   Really?

ARTHUR   Yes. I'm attracted to housekeepers in general. Especially in hotels. There's a woman in your room, wearing a uniform. It's a sexually charged situation

NORMAN   You're like that guy from France.

ARTHUR   Strauss-Kahn? No. He forced her. That I don't get. I mean, at least ask. Put a move on her. Buy her a drink. Offer to vacuum. Something.

NORMAN   And how do you force someone? It's hard enough to have sex if it's consensual . . . You know, for me . . . Anyway, here's the thing. Dad was giving them money and he said he was going to talk to you about it, but, tragically, he never got the chance.

ARTHUR   Dad was going to talk to me about taking care of them?

NORMAN   Yeah, well, makes sense. You're the guy with the money. Why wouldn't he?

ARTHUR   I got all that money . . .

NORMAN   You got the money.

ARTHUR   Okay, that's obviously bullshit. Nice try.

NORMAN   It's not bullshit!

ARTHUR   "He never got the chance?" . . . Norman, you disappoint me. There's no way I'm taking care of them.

NORMAN   We have to do something.

ARTHUR   She's your maid.

NORMAN   My maid?! She comes once a week and that's only because I'm doing her a favor. You know my financial situation. And by the way, lest I remind you—Ta-dah! (*pointing to Gloria*) That's what I got going! So it all falls on me? Mom and Diego?! I get the check and the tip?

Brenda enters.

BRENDA   What's going on?

NORMAN   He won't take her.

BRENDA   He won't and you will?

NORMAN   What can I do?

BRENDA   You're choosing your mother over me?

NORMAN   I'm not choosing anybody! I'm trying to be a good son!

BRENDA   How about trying to be a decent husband?

NORMAN   Look, it was a dying request from my father! I can't ignore that. You wouldn't want me if I was like that.

Arthur slinks out. Norman points to Arthur.

Like him!

BRENDA   That's where you're wrong. You could do with a little more Arthur and a little less Norman!

NORMAN   That's the most insulting thing anyone's ever said to me!

BRENDA   Go cry to Mommy about it!

NORMAN   No, that's the most insulting!

Brenda leaves. Gloria comes stomping in.

GLORIA   Norman.

NORMAN What?

GLORIA Your wife stormed out of here without so much as a "Good-bye, Gloria. So sorry for your loss. If there's anything I can do . . ." Nothing. I have no use for her.

She exits, just as Arthur reenters, steaming.

ARTHUR What the fuck? What did you say to Jessica?

NORMAN I didn't say anything. I complimented her on the eulogy.

ARTHUR Oh, compliment? She didn't write the eulogy?

NORMAN I never said that.

ARTHUR Well she's crying. She said you told her she didn't write it.

NORMAN Nope! Nope, nope . . . I never said it. I implied it.

ARTHUR You're a fucking asshole, you know that?

NORMAN Oh I'm an asshole? I didn't ghostwrite a eulogy for my daughter, then brag about how wonderful she is and watch her take credit for it.

ARTHUR I didn't write it and you're just jealous because it was better than yours. I know you. You wanted your eulogy to be the best. It had to be the best . . . ! (*he storms off, then O.S.:*) Come on, Jessica, we're leaving!

NORMAN I wrote mine! It was better! It was the fucking best! IT WAS PROFOUND!

Curtain

END OF ACT ONE

ACT TWO

Norman's house. SR, a kitchen area with a right-angle island counter that looks onto the great room, which contains a comfortable sofa and chair The front door is UC. There are also doors DL and DR. Brenda's touches are everywhere, from the plants to the artwork, to the shabby chic decor. She made a beautiful home for Norman—and apparently his mother.

Norman enters, dragging heavy luggage, followed by Gloria.

GLORIA   I just do not understand why you have to drive so close to the other cars. What's the hurry? Why the rush? We were only going from my house to your house. You know what else? I don't even need all this stuff. It's not like I'm going anywhere.

NORMAN (*covering his face*)   Oh my God. You know what you should think about? . . . A cruise. People love cruises.

GLORIA   Are you kidding? The toilets don't ever work. That's all I need . . . Drek boat.

NORMAN   It happened one time. They fixed that.

GLORIA   The boat probably still stinks.

NORMAN   Do you think that's the only boat? It's a great trip. Goes to all these different ports.

GLORIA   What, Haiti? That's not on my bucket list.

NORMAN   Who said anything about Haiti?

GLORIA   And I'm not going to Puerto Rico.

FABIANA (*enters from the bedroom*)   What's wrong with Puerto Rico?

GLORIA   Fabiana? Oh that's right. I forgot you work here.

FABIANA   You have a problem with Puerto Rico?

GLORIA   No more so than the average person.

FABIANA (*under her breath*)   Pendeja.

Gloria goes into her bedroom.

NORMAN   Hey, what's with the attitude?

FABIANA   It's not my attitude. It's her attitude!

NORMAN   She had a bad experience there.

FABIANA   What bad experience?

NORMAN   She couldn't get a cabana. It was a disaster.

FABIANA   I don't work for her anymore. I don't have to be nice.

NORMAN   Yes you do . . . Look, I know you don't like her. It's understandable. You're jealous because my father was married to her.

FABIANA   Jealous?! Your father loved me, not her. I work for you, not her. I'm not going to let her boss me around like she used to.

GLORIA   Fabiana, would you put up some coffee?

FABIANA   One second.

GLORIA   And I'd love a biscuit with that. A nice warm biscuit with a little butter. Delicious! (*she goes back to her bedroom*)

FABIANA (*to Norman*)   A biscuit?

NORMAN   It's sort of like a combination of bread and a cookie.

FABIANA   I know what a biscuit is! (*to Gloria*) We don't have biscuits.

NORMAN   No biscuits!

Gloria reeneters.

GLORIA   What kind of house doesn't have biscuits? Buy some biscuits.(*she returns to her room*)

NORMAN   Ah, shut the hell up!

Brenda enters.

Hey! You're moving back?

BRENDA   Is your mother here?

NORMAN   She just got here.

BRENDA   Then no, I'm not. I came for my body pillow. (*she heads for the bedroom, then turns back abruptly*) August 7, 2006.

NORMAN   Oh, here we go.

BRENDA   It was a Monday. We had dinner with your family at Fratelli's. Your mother, your father, Rose, Harry, and Stewie. It took a month to get the reservation. Of course, they didn't like anything on the menu and they all ordered spaghetti and meatballs, which wasn't even on the menu. I got in an argument with Stewie, who was being impossible about it, and called him a dickhead. And then he called me a cunt. A cunt! And you just sat there! You didn't even support me! You took his side!

NORMAN   You called him a dickhead!

BRENDA   Cunt is much worse than dickhead!

NORMAN   Dickhead is the cunt equivalent!

BRENDA   A dickhead is just a jerk.A cunt is a vicious, miserable hag.

NORMAN   I was doing it more by body parts.

BRENDA   You didn't support me then and you're not supporting me now!

NORMAN   You can't go around calling people dickheads!

BRENDA   . . . Do you know why we never have sex?

NORMAN   Do I know why we never have sex? . . . Is it because you don't want to ruin the friendship?

BRENDA   Because you spend so much time in the bathroom before you come in at night that I lose all desire and fall asleep!

NORMAN   I need to do my nightly ablutions.

BRENDA   Every night you're in that bathroom for a half hour, flossing and water pik-ing and brushing and sudsing and moisturizing and gum stimming!!

NORMAN   My dentist says I have the gums of a thirty-year-old man!

BRENDA   The point is, whenever I'm in the mood, you're not there! WHY CAN'T YOU JUST BRUSH YOUR TEETH AND GET INTO BED LIKE A NORMAL PERSON?!

NORMAN   Why couldn't you put that scarf on once? Just once?!

GLORIA (*O.S. shouting*)   —Norman? Norman?!

NORMAN (*to Gloria*)   WHAT?!

GLORIA (*O.S.*)   Come here!

NORMAN   You come here!

Gloria enters.

GLORIA   I can't find the remote . . . Oh, hello, Brenda. Very nice to see you.

BRENDA   Hello, Gloria. I hope you two will be very happy together.

To Norman.

And it is walk the talk. I did some research! (*she storms out*)

GLORIA   What's with her?

NORMAN (*calling after Brenda*)   Hey, you forgot your body pillow!

Gloria goes back to her room as Fabiana enters.

FABIANA (*to Norman*)   So Mr. Drexel, did you talk to your brother about Diego?

NORMAN   Yes, I have. He won't give me anything. How much was my father giving you?

FABIANA   Thirty thousand a year. Not a lot for me and your brother.

NORMAN   Thirty thousand? I don't have that kind of money.

FABIANA   Your mother does.

NORMAN   My mother? She's even cheaper than Arthur. She's not even leaving us anything. She's giving it all to Hadassah.

FABIANA   Who's she?

NORMAN   Her sister.

FABIANA   Well you can explain all this to Diego. He's coming here to pick me up.

NORMAN   Here?

FABIANA   Any minute.

Gloria reenters.

GLORIA   Fabiana? Where's my coffee? And you know what I just thought of? Cinnamon toast! You can never go wrong with cinnamon toast!

The doorbell rings.

I'll get it.

She opens the door and standing before her is . . .

SIDNEY!!!

And with that, she faints.

Blackout

Norman and Fabiana in the great room, moments later. Gloria is out on the couch. Norman and Fabiana are hovering.

NORMAN   Boy, I hope she's okay.

FABIANA   I don't think she hurt herself.

NORMAN   I mean mentally. She thinks she just saw her dead husband. They look exactly the same.

FABIANA   It's astounding . . . We gotta wake her up.

NORMAN (*trying to rouse her*)   Ma, *Matlock's* on! . . . Ma, the house is filthy. There are dirty dishes in the sink. The tub's disgusting. Schmutz all over and company's coming. Company!

FABIANA   That's not working.

NORMAN   I've got another idea . . . (*crouching over Gloria*) . . . Mom, meet my new girlfriend, Habeeba. She's from Gaza! She's a member of Hamas! I'm going to visit her home next week. Did you hear what I said, Ma? I'm going to Gaza! GAZA!

Gloria finally stirs.

GLORIA   Norman . . . I saw him. I saw Daddy.

NORMAN   You did?

GLORIA   Yes, he came to the front door. He was here. I saw Daddy. But he was very young. Looked exactly like he did the day we first met—when he came out of an elevator in his army uniform and bumped into me.

NORMAN   Maybe you should go lie down in your room, get some rest.

GLORIA   You don't believe me. He's trying to tell me something. You think I'm crazy.

NORMAN   It was probably someone who looked like Dad.

GLORIA No one could look that much like him. Same eyes, same hair, same expression. I know your father.

Norman leads her back to the bedroom and shoves her inside, then reemerges, as Fabiana removes a bowl of food from the fridge.

NORMAN This is not going to end well.

FABIANA I made meatballs and spaghetti. Want some?

NORMAN Meatballs and spaghetti?! I'll take a plate.

The doorbell rings.

NORMAN That's Arthur. I'll get it.

Fabiana exits SL as Norman lets in Arthur.

. . . Oh, hello.

ARTHUR What's going on? Why all the drama?

NORMAN Diego, Fabiana's son, stopped by. He's a dead ringer for Dad at that age. Mom saw him and fainted.

ARTHUR Where is she?

NORMAN In Natalie's room.

ARTHUR Hey! So get this. I had dinner last night and recommended the veal piccata to the—do you know what veal piccata is?

NORMAN Yeah, yeah, it's the lemon one.

ARTHUR Right, so I recommended it to the guy sitting next to me. He orders it, doesn't like it, and blames me. We got into a big fight!

NORMAN That's fascinating. Have you thought anymore about our talk?

ARTHUR Our talk?

NORMAN Yeah, about helping out with Diego.

ARTHUR (*ignores him, heads for the kitchen*) Oh, that's why you called me? No, I haven't thought about it and I won't think about it.

NORMAN So it's not just "Nothing for the dead," it's also "Nothing for the living"? Hey . . . Maybe there's one thing you could do for me.

ARTHUR What is it?

NORMAN Well, you know, Brenda left me . . . Thank you very much.

ARTHUR Ah-ha! See?

NORMAN I want Michelle's number.

ARTHUR Why?

NORMAN I can sit through an hour dinner, no problem.

ARTHUR That's very bold of you, Norman.

NORMAN I'm just trying to be more like you, Arthur. I would think you'd encourage that.

ARTHUR I've never seen you like this.

NORMAN That day in the hospital, I was so jealous of Dad. I wished it was me who was dying.

ARTHUR I can't do it.

NORMAN Why not?

ARTHUR Doesn't feel right

NORMAN Hey, I've got your wacked out mother in there for life! For the rest of her life. In there. Every day! Every meal. Shopping. Doctor visits. Listening to her raving about bialys. My life is over! And I have no idea how I'm going to send this kid to college.

ARTHUR   You don't have to do that.

NORMAN   I know I don't have to, but it's Dad's kid. He's our brother. I would do it for you. So could you not do one thing for me? One small thing that costs you nothing?

ARTHUR   I don't really want you dating her.

NORMAN   Well you know what? I know where she works. I'll call her anyway.

ARTHUR   She wouldn't go out with you.

NORMAN   Why not?

ARTHUR   Because you have no game. You're clumsy and awkward and inappropriate. You couldn't make a move if your life depended on it. Your dream date is a woman breaking into your house and sitting on your penis!

NORMAN   Who wouldn't want that? Anyway . . . I've got moves! I've got plenty of moves.

ARTHUR   Fine, go make all the moves you want. Let me know how that works out. (*he starts to leave*)

NORMAN   That's right, get out! And by the way, we're done.

ARTHUR   Fine with me.

NORMAN   Yeah, fine with me too!

As soon as Arthur exits, Norman picks up the phone and dials.

. . . Um, yes, I'd like to speak with Michelle please . . . Oh, hey . . . It's Norman Drexel, Arthur's brother . . . Hi . . . So Arthur told me you guys broke up and I was wondering . . . if maybe you want to go out and get a beverage of some kind . . . A frothy latte . . . A lovely Dr. Pepper . . . Perhaps a 5-hour Energy? . . . Oh, well she moved out . . . She's growing and I'm not . . . Really? That sounds great . . . Fantastic! I'm very excited.

Unbeknownst to Norman, Brenda enters.

Still on phone:

See you Saturday. *(he hangs up)*

BRENDA   See who on Saturday?

NORMAN   Hey!

BRENDA   Hey . . .

She goes into the bedroom, as Norman grabs a bowl of the spaghetti. She then returns moments later with her body pillow.

BRENDA   Who are you seeing on Saturday?

NORMAN   Oh, I'm meeting with the head of the block association. Mark Tobin. There've been some prowlers and . . . we're going to talk about it. I might have to do some neighborhood watch duties.

BRENDA   Well you go get 'em, Batman. I'm sure you'll be quite a deterrent.

She starts to head out. Norman holds up his plate of food.

NORMAN   Do you want some meatballs and spaghetti?

BRENDA   Okay.

As Fabiana reenters, Brenda takes the plate and hurls it at the painting, then exits without a word.

FABIANA   . . . I'm not cleaning that up.

NORMAN   Oh for God's sake! She's nuts! *(he grabs a sponge and starts to wipe up)*

FABIANA   How was your talk with Arthur?

NORMAN   . . . That bastard! He's so goddamn selfish. Won't give me anything . . . I don't know where I'm going to get that kind of money.

FABIANA   So what are you saying?! Diego's going to starve? Oh my God! How am I going to pay for college and his Pilates and his improv classes?

NORMAN   I don't know.

FABIANA   You don't know.

NORMAN   No.

FABIANA   . . . Well I know one way.

Norman puts the sponge down, gives her his full attention.

NORMAN   You do?

FABIANA   . . . Yes, I do.

NORMAN   What is it?

FABIANA   What if Sidney tells your mother to give me the money?

NORMAN   What are you talking about?

FABIANA   Listen to me . . . She thinks Diego is Sidney, so we have Diego tell her as Sidney.

NORMAN   That's crazy.

FABIANA   Why? We just have "Sidney" pay her a little visit tonight.

NORMAN   Oh, it's impossible. Even if I agreed to it, what about Diego? He would never do it and he couldn't do it.

FABIANA   Of course he could. Sidney and Diego spent a lot of time together. Diego can imitate everybody. He even does Ben Affleck from "The Town" with the Boston accent.

NORMAN   He does Ben Affleck from "The Town"?

FABIANA   He does Ben Affleck and he does a perfect Sidney voice.

NORMAN   And he would come here and do that?

FABIANA   Of course.

NORMAN   Interesting.

FABIANA   Yes it is.

Gloria wearily reenters.

GLORIA   First the Oriole and then he appears at the door. I'm not crazy, Norman. I'm not crazy . . . Pick up some biscuits tomorrow. (*she returns to her bedroom*)

Norman turns back to Fabiana, seeing her in a new light.

NORMAN   How soon can he get here?

Blackout

Gloria's bedroom. It's 3 a.m. and she's sound asleep. The window is open. It's a rainy night and we hear a crack of thunder, followed by a flash of lightning, which casts a supernatural glow on the room, and reveals Diego, who's sitting on a chair next to her bed, wearing Sidney's old army uniform.

DIEGO (*whispers singsongy, à la Sidney*)   Gloria . . . Glor-i-a . . .

No response.

Gloria—Gloria!

She stirs.

GLORIA   . . . Sidney?

DIEGO   Yes, it's me, my darling.

GLORIA   Oh. I knew that was you earlier. What are you doing here so late? You have to pop in? You could've given me a heart attack.

DIEGO   Next time I'll text!

GLORIA   So . . . you're dead.

DIEGO   I'm dead.

GLORIA   How is it?

DIEGO   Honestly, if I knew I was going to feel this good, I would've killed myself years ago.

GLORIA   Really.

DIEGO   Oh yeah. And if I had to quibble—and I don't have to, no one's holding a gun to my head, saying, "Quibble!"—It's a little too bright. No nighttime. It's like Norway in the summer. So if you don't like bright, this is not the place for you.

GLORIA   You look very handsome in your uniform.

DIEGO (*lapsing into normal voice*)   Thank you. (*realizing, clears throat*) I mean . . . thank you.

GLORIA   So when I die, am I also going to be nineteen?

DIEGO   You don't know until you get here. Some people are ten, others eighty. I got lucky . . . Look, Gloria, I don't have much time. We have a few things to discuss.

GLORIA   Like what?

DIEGO   I want you to give some money to a few people,

GLORIA   What people?

DIEGO   Well . . . our housekeeper, Fabiana, for one.

GLORIA   Fabiana? Why the hell do you want me to give her money? She hasn't worked for us in ten years . . . And she's a real pain in the ass, that one. Very fresh.

DIEGO   Well it's not an easy job. Maybe she wanted to do other things, but never had the opportunity.

GLORIA   Oh I'm so sorry if the housekeeping got in the way of her being an engineer.

DIEGO   . . . Anyway, I want you to go see Jay Leventhal. I'd like to give her thirty thousand a year. I left you plenty . . . It doesn't matter.

GLORIA   Are you out of your mind? What is this? You die and suddenly you're a big sport?

DIEGO   Look, her kid wants to go to college and medical school.

GLORIA   If that kid's a doctor, I'm a pirate . . .

DIEGO   Gloria.

GLORIA   If you really want me to, I'll do it.

DIEGO   Don't forget to get it in writing, just in case.

GLORIA   Are you sure about this?

DIEGO   Just do it, Gloria!

GLORIA   Okay . . . Oh, before I forget, did you tell Harry when you were in the hospital that he could have your Rolex?

DIEGO (*confused*)   . . . Yes. I did.

GLORIA   That's so unlike you.

DIEGO   Well, I was dying. A momentary lapse . . . Anyway, I'd better get to my heaven meeting. They penalize you. You know, because I'm new.

She pulls back the covers, making room for him.

GLORIA   Come here. Relax a little. You went through a death. That must be exhausting.

DIEGO   I'm not tired. I feel like I'm nineteen.

GLORIA   I know.

She grabs his hand, pulls him down onto the bed.

Come here, Sidney.

DIEGO   What are you doing?

GLORIA (*all over him*)   Oh, Sidney . . . My God. Oh Sidney.

DIEGO (*trying to get her off*)   Gloria . . . Gloria.

GLORIA   Oh my God. Look at you. Look at you.

She smothers him with kisses. Diego continues to protest, but to no avail.

Blackout

SCENE 4

*Norman's kitchen, the next morning. Gloria enters with a heretofore
unseen bounce in her step. The romp with young Sidney has
transformed her.*

GLORIA (*singing from* "My Fair Lady")   Bed, bed, I couldn't go to
bed . . .

Norman enters.

My head's too light to try to set it down!

NORMAN   Good morning!

GLORIA (*still singing*)   Sleep, sleep, I couldn't sleep tonight. Not
for all the jewels in the crown . . .

NORMAN   Well aren't you the merry widow.

GLORIA   Norman, I've been doing some thinking.

NORMAN   Yes.

GLORIA   And I've decided that I want to give Fabiana some
money.

NORMAN   Mother . . . ? Mother! My God, that's so generous of
you.

GLORIA   Yes, isn't it? Quite remarkable. It feels good. It happens
to feel very good.

NORMAN   I bet it does.

GLORIA   Remember how Scrooge felt when he changed at the
end? Kind of like that. But don't get me wrong, I'm no Scrooge.

NORMAN   But this is wonderful. Look at you—you're smiling! I
don't think I've ever seen your teeth before. You happen to have
nice teeth. Did you know that?

GLORIA   One of my best features . . . Anyway, I'm off. I'm going
to the bank, followed by a little shopping.

NORMAN   What are you going to get?

GLORIA   Oh some . . . underpinnings.

NORMAN   Underpinnings?

GLORIA   Just some lady stuff.

Fabiana enters cheerfully, holding a bag.

FABIANA   I got biscuits!

GLORIA   Thank you, Fabiana.

FABIANA   And they have cinnamon on them.

GLORIA   Cinnamon biscuits! Where did you find that?

FABIANA   I made them! Take a bite.

GLORIA (*trying one*)   Mmm . . . out of this world!

*She exits to her bedroom, humming "I Could've Danced All Night".
As soon as the bedroom door closes, Norman breaks into* My Fair
Lady's *"Tonight, Old Boy, You Did It".*

NORMAN (*singing, while sharing a celebratory victory dance with
Fabiana*)   Tonight, old man, you did it! You did it! You did it! You
said that you would do it and, indeed, you did!

FABIANA   Thank you!

NORMAN   Boy, you're right about Diego! That kid's something.

FABIANA   I told you . . . Mr. Drexel, my friend says I should get
everything in writing as soon as possible. Your mother's old. What
if something happens?

NORMAN   Nothing is going to happen. I'll take care of it
Monday.

FABIANA   No, do it today!

Gloria reenters from the bedroom with her purse and the Rolex.

GLORIA Oh, FYI, your dad really did tell Harry he could have the Rolex.

NORMAN Oh, FYI? He didn't. Okay?

GLORIA He did.

NORMAN (*emphatic*) Mom . . . he didn't.

GLORIA Norman, trust me, okay? I know.

NORMAN No you don't know. First off, Dad promised me that watch.

GLORIA Nope, he gave it to Harry. Anyway, I'm going there now to drop it off.

NORMAN No you're not! It's mine! Give me that!

Brenda and Natalie enter. They observe Gloria and Norman fighting over the watch for a few beats. Then:

BRENDA What did you do?!

NORMAN What?

NATALIE (*as cockney Eliza the entire scene*) Greg and I had a 'uge row! I moved out!

NORMAN Can you talk normal please?

NATALIE When 'e ask you for your blessin', you tol' 'im you dint want us gettin' married! I said it didn't matter, but by then, 'e realized that this family is nothin' but a bunch of bloomin' idiots and dint wan' anything to do with the likes'o me! Why would you do that?

NORMAN It was a joke!

NATALIE (*looking to Brenda for help*) Mum!

BRENDA A joke?!

NORMAN I was just getting back at him.

NATALIE Gettin' back at 'im for what?

NORMAN For telling me to tip the doctor.

BRENDA What?!

NORMAN He told me to tip the doctor.

NATALIE Tip the doctor?

BRENDA Who tips the doctor?

NORMAN No one tips the doctor.

BRENDA Did *you* tip the doctor?

NORMAN No, but I tried.

BRENDA (*incredulous*) You tried to tip the doctor?

NATALIE 'Cause Greg tol' you to?

NORMAN I didn't want to shirk my tipping responsibilities! You know how anxious I am about missing tips. I'm so sorry! Let me call him.

BRENDA You've done enough.

NATALIE It's over. (*she storms out*)

BRENDA (*to Norman*) You've really raised your stupidity bar . . . Which was already set pretty high.

GLORIA Don't you call my son stupid!

BRENDA You call him stupid all the time!

GLORIA I'm allowed to! You can leave.

BRENDA It's my house!

GLORIA We paid for it!

BRENDA We paid you back!

GLORIA Half!

BRENDA (*to Norman*)   Half?

Norman shrugs.

Unbelievable!

Gloria notices the blank space on the wall and pauses in front of it.

GLORIA   . . . Where's my painting?

BRENDA   It's on loan to the Met. (*she leaves.*)

GLORIA   What the hell is wrong with you? You tried to tip the doctor?

Norman shrugs.

Okay, I'll see you later. What do you want for dinner? I'm cooking . . .

NORMAN   Surprise me.

GLORIA   Will do. *Buenos dias*, Fabiana!

FABIANA   *Buenos dias!*

GLORIA   *Buenos dias*, Norman!

NORMAN   *Buenos dias, mi madre.*

Gloria exits. Norman groans.

FABIANA   I wish there was something I could do for you, Mr. Drexel.

NORMAN   There isn't. I just want my life back. (*he heads to his bedroom and closes the door*)

A few beats and he enthusiastically reemerges, raising his pointer finger with an idea.

Blackout

Norman's great room. It's a little after midnight. There's a tap on the front door. Norman emerges from his bedroom in nightclothes and crosses to answer it. Diego's back, in uniform.

NORMAN   Hey, Pops.

DIEGO *(glumly)*   Hi.

NORMAN   What's wrong?

DIEGO   Do I really have to do this?

NORMAN   Yeah. What's the big deal? Just do what you did last night.

DIEGO *(contemplating)*   Yeah . . . Is there no other way?

NORMAN   If you knew my situation you'd understand. All you have to do is go in there and tell my mother that she's in the wrong house. She's supposed to be at Arthur's. Got it?

DIEGO   Yeah.

NORMAN   Speaking of last night, that was incredible what you did. I don't think it's an overstatement to say that you'll remember what happened in there for the rest of your life. Not a day will go by that you won't think of it as a truly magical experience. Now get in there and do your thing.

Diego heads toward Gloria's room.

Hey.

Diego turns back to Norman, who salutes him. With that, Diego trudges off into Gloria's room.

So long Ma! It's been swell having you!

He picks up the phone, dials, and waits.

Buona sera. Do you deliver? . . . Fantastic! All right, I'd like a big, big order of meatballs and spaghetti with plenty of gluten. And

how about a tiramisu for dessert? Do we love that? And what the
hell. A bottle of Chianti . . . I'm celebrating. My mother's moving
out—knock on wood . . . You got any wood over there? Give
it a couple of taps . . . Hey, let me ask you a question. Is it walk
the walk, talk the talk, or walk the talk? . . . Oh, I completely
disagree . . . Okay, it's 212 8th Street . . . Drexel . . . Thanks. See
you soon. *Arrivederci!* (*he hangs up the phone, then walks into the
kitchen*)

DIEGO (*O.S. screaming*)   Gloria! Gloria! (*he comes running out
in his underwear*) Oh my god! Something's wrong! Something's
wrong!

NORMAN   What the fuck?!

DIEGO   Something happened. Call an ambulance!

NORMAN   What happened?! Why are you in your underwear?!

DIEGO (*unable to come up with anything*)   Because . . .

NORMAN   Because . . . ?

DIEGO   Because . . .

NORMAN   Because . . . ? Because . . . ?

DIEGO (*spitting it out*)   Because I FUCKED her!

NORMAN   You what?!

DIEGO   I fucked her!

NORMAN   You fucked my mother?!!!

DIEGO   Yes!

NORMAN   Why?!!

DIEGO   She wanted me to! I didn't want to. Call 911. I think she
had a stroke.

NORMAN   Are you insane? (*dialing the phone*) . . . Hello . . . Yes, I need an ambulance. 212 8th Street . . . I don't know. Sex-induced stroke? (*he hangs up*) You fucked my mother?!

DIEGO   I'm sorry.

NORMAN   Should we go in there?

DIEGO   No! She's out! Don't go in there!

NORMAN   I have to!

He heads toward the bedroom.

DIEGO   Norman, don't!

Norman opens the door and quickly slams it shut, screaming as if he's trying to erase the vision from his mind.

NORMAN   She's naked! She's completely naked! Oh that's disturbing . . . I didn't want to see that!

DIEGO   I told you not to go in!

NORMAN   You couldn't cover her up?!

DIEGO   I'm sorry! I panicked!

NORMAN   . . . Is she dead?

DIEGO   I don't think so.

NORMAN   Did you tell her you wanted her to live with Arthur?

DIEGO   Never got to it.

NORMAN   Oh, you never got to it? Never got to it?! You were too busy, no doubt? What the hell happened?

DIEGO   I can't tell you! It'll haunt you for the rest of your life.

NORMAN   You think what I just saw isn't going to haunt me? . . . I gotta make a call . . .

Blackout

Norman picks up the phone and dials. Lights out on Norman's living room.

Then, over a darkened stage:

NORMAN   Yes, hello! there's been an emergency! Something happened to my mother . . . I think she had a stroke and the ambulance is coming, so I have to cancel my order . . . What do you mean you're going to charge me? . . . All right, well I'm not going to pay for the tiramisu . . . Nobody touched it . . . Did you knock on wood, by the way? . . . Yeah, I didn't think so. This is all your fault.

SCENE 6

The same hospital lounge from Act 1. Norman is sitting on the couch, waiting. After a few beats, the elevator doors open and Fabiana steps out. Norman is surprised to see her.

NORMAN What are you doing?

FABIANA What am I doing? I want to know what's going on and I'm not leaving until I find out!

NORMAN I don't know. I haven't spoken to the doctor yet. He's in there with her now.

FABIANA Oh, this is so upsetting. This has been very hard on Diego.

NORMAN Oh, it's been hard on Diego . . .

FABIANA Don't blame Diego for this! You're the one who made him come back! He didn't know he was going to have *chingando* with your mother!

NORMAN He told you?!

FABIANA Of course. He tells me everything. We're very close.

NORMAN What kind of son did you raise who has sex with the elderly? What is he, sick?

FABIANA No, he's not sick! He's nineteen. That's what they do!

NORMAN I didn't jump geriatrics when I was nineteen!

Doctor Meyers exits Gloria's room.

NORMAN Hey, Dr. Meyers . . . This is my housekeeper, Fabiana . . .

FABIANA Hello. Nice to meet you.

DR. MEYERS How do you do?

NORMAN So what's going on?

DR. MEYERS   Well, we suspect she had a ventricular tachycardia.

FABIANA   A what?

DR. MEYERS   It's an arrhythmia, where the heart is vibrating like jello and blood doesn't get to the brain.

NORMAN   Vibrating like jello.

DR. MEYERS   I expect her to regain consciousness, but the truth is, it's not a certainty.

NORMAN   What would you say the odds are?

DR. MEYERS   Fifty-fifty.

NORMAN   Hmm . . . Okay.

DR. MEYERS   I just wonder what could've triggered it. She doesn't have a cardiac history, so it must've been some pretty unusual event. Can you think of anything that might have provoked it?

NORMAN   No, I can't think of anything.

DR. MEYERS   Okay. Well, we'll just continue to monitor the situation.

NORMAN   Great. Thanks a lot.

A few beats, as Dr. Meyers waits, much like a bellman before leaving a hotel room. Norman is befuddled, then finally removes some bills from his pocket.

There you go.

DR. MEYERS (*takes the money*)   Thanks so much. (*he exits*)

FABIANA   Not a certainty? What if she doesn't wake up? Then I'm out of luck!

NORMAN   You're out of luck? What about her? . . . What if we've killed her?

FABIANA   We?! You! You!

NORMAN   You! The whole Diego/Sidney thing was your idea. "He'll be Sidney! He'll be Sidney!"

FABIANA   . . . Oh Sidney . . . If only Sidney were here.

Unbeknownst to Norman and Fabiana, the elevator doors open and Diego steps out.

DIEGO   Hey. How's she doing? Is she still unconscious?

Norman and Fabiana turn and see Diego.

NORMAN   Sidney!

He and Fabiana rush over to Diego, who immediately presses the elevator button and runs back inside, but Norman catches him in time and pulls him out.

DIEGO   . . . No! No!

Fabiana blocks the elevator door.

NORMAN   All you gotta do—and you're the only one who can do it—is go in there and tell my mother that it's not her time.

DIEGO   No, please! Don't make me! I can't! Please! Please! Please! (*he looks to Fabiana for help*)

FABIANA   I can't help you, kid.

Diego finally concedes and allows Norman to walk him to Gloria's door.

NORMAN   . . . And after you wake her, try to control yourself.

As Diego dejectedly enters Gloria's room, Norman takes out his phone.

You know what I'm going to do for you? I'm gonna get the lawyer, Jay Leventhal. We'll work it out right now.

FABIANA   Oh, that's so nice of you, Mr. Drexel.

NORMAN (*as he texts*)   You know, Fabiana, for the last ten years you've been calling me Mr. Drescoll. That's not my name. It's Drexel.

FABIANA   That's what I'm saying.

NORMAN   Nope, not even close. You're saying Drescoll. It's DREX-el. Drexel . . . What's my name?

FABIANA   Norman.

The elevator doors open and Uncle Stewie hurries out, holding a bouquet of flowers. Norman intercepts, stepping between him and Gloria's room.

STEWIE   I came as soon as I heard!

NORMAN   Uncle Stewie! What are you doing?

STEWIE   Marty Simon told me he saw you coming into the hospital. First one, then the other? I can't believe it.

NORMAN (*with rising anxiety*)   You can't be here! Anyway, someone's in there.

STEWIE   Who? Harry?! Again?! I'm going in!

NORMAN   No, you can't!

STEWIE   Fuck him! Once is enough, Norman! It's not fair!

NORMAN   It's not him!

Stewie tries to shove Norman aside. They grapple. Norman forces him back toward the elevator. Fabiana pushes the elevator button, then goes inside to hold the door open.

STEWIE   I don't want to hurt you, Norman!

NORMAN   It's not a good time!

He finally shoves Stewie in and Fabiana pushes the button to close the doors.

FABIANA (*to Stewie, as the doors begin to close*)   Are you okay?

STEWIE   No.

The doors close and Stewie and Fabiana are gone. Norman breathes a sigh of relief. A few beats, before the elevator doors open again, revealing Jay and Michelle.

NORMAN   Oh my god . . .

MICHELLE   Hello.

JAY   You guys know each other. I needed a notary.

NORMAN   Right! Of course. Were you already here in the hospital?

JAY   Unfortunately. Where's your mother?

NORMAN   She's not awake yet, but it's imminent.

JAY   All right. I've got someone else on this floor. I'll be right back.

He leaves down the hallway. Michelle takes a seat on the couch. Norman paces, looking anxiously toward Gloria's room.

MICHELLE   So is this considered a date?

NORMAN   Well I haven't showered, shaved, or gargled, so I don't think so.

MICHELLE   Does your brother know you called me?

NORMAN   No. I asked him if he minded and he said he did . . .

MICHELLE   Did he tell you why he stopped seeing me?

NORMAN   Yes.

MICHELLE   I don't know what his problem is. It didn't seem like it was that big of a deal. How did you feel about it?

NORMAN   I thought it was—and I've never used this word before—hot.

Michelle smiles. He's transfixed.

In fact, I haven't been able to stop thinking about it. (*then he goes for the boob*)

MICHELLE   What are you doing?! (*she slaps his hand away*)

NORMAN   Not okay?

MICHELLE   Not okay! You can't just do that!

NORMAN   My father did.

MICHELLE   Well he was dying!

NORMAN   . . . I've been married. Same thing!

Fabiana steps out of the elevator, just as Diego emerges from Gloria's room. Michelle heads to the elevator and exits.

DIEGO   She's up.

Norman and Fabiana shower Diego with praise.

NORMAN   Oh my God! Good going! That's fantastic!

FABIANA   I'm so proud of you!

Just as Jay returns, Norman notices Michelle in the elevator.

NORMAN   I'm sorry! I'm sorry!

The elevator doors close.

FABIANA   What happened?

NORMAN   The notary left.

FABIANA   Why?

NORMAN   I touched her *teta*.

FABIANA   Right here? In the hospital?!

NORMAN   Right here in the hospital.

FABIANA You know what you need, Norman? A life coach. (*she pushes the elevator button*) And more importantly, you gotta get your wife back.

She and Diego enter the elevator. As the doors close:

. . . And we're out of laundry detergent.

JAY . . . What the hell?

NORMAN I couldn't help it. I was possessed.

JAY Hey, everybody is. She's worked for me for twelve years. It's not easy.

NORMAN I can imagine.

JAY So . . . how'd it feel?

NORMAN Pretty good. Pretty . . . pretty . . . pretty . . . pretty good.

JAY Well what do you want to do now?

NORMAN As soon as she gets out of here, first chance I get, I'll bring her to the office.

JAY (*standing up to leave*) All right.

NORMAN Hey . . . You're divorced, right?

JAY Yes, but I'd like to get married again someday.

NORMAN You would?

JAY Sure . . . I don't want to die alone. I want to live alone, I just don't want to die alone.

NORMAN Right. Although my father just died with ten people around him and I think he might've been better off alone.

JAY (*while getting on the elevator*) Well, maybe with your family . . .

Doors close.

NORMAN   Yeah . . . maybe with my family . . .

He ponders this, lost in thought, as the lights go down on the lounge. Lights up on Gloria's hospital room. Gloria is in bed, as the Nurse tends to her.

NURSE   You're doing much better, Mrs. Drexel.

GLORIA   Thank you. You've been very helpful . . . Do you wear you hair like that all the time or just for work?

NURSE   No, this is how I wear it.

GLORIA   I see you're not married. You might want to think about the hair.

Norman enters.

NORMAN   Hey, Mom.

GLORIA   Norman.

NORMAN   How are you feeling?

GLORIA   Surprisingly well. Where's Brenda?

NORMAN   I wish I knew.

The Nurse exits, as Natalie and Greg enter.

NATALIE   Hi, Grandma!

GREG   Hey, Mrs. Drexel. Hey, Norman.

NORMAN   Hey, look at this! You made up?

NATALIE   We made up.

NORMAN   And you're talking like your old self again.

NATALIE   My friends had a Facetime intervention.

GREG   Hey, Norman. I'm so sorry about all this . . . but my Dad really does tip doctors.

NORMAN You know what? I'm sorry, because I just tipped one ten minutes ago.

GREG You see!

He hugs Norman.

NORMAN (*mid-hug*) Not necessary.

There's a knock on the door. It's Stewie, Rose, and Harry, who has bruises and bandages on his face. His left arm is in a sling.

ROSE Gloria!

NORMAN What the hell?

ROSE These hoodlums beat him up and took his Rolex!

NORMAN How did that happen?

ROSE Because he was asking for it, showing the watch off to strangers in the parking lot.

HARRY I wasn't showing it off!

ROSE Idiot. If it wasn't for Stewie here, he could've been killed. Stewie jumped in and they ran away. But they got the Rolex.

STEWIE To tell you the truth, I didn't even know who it was.

HARRY So if you'd known it was me, you would've let me get beat up?

STEWIE If I'd known it was you, I would've helped them.

NORMAN (*looking at his phone*) Oh my God.

NATALIE What is it?

NORMAN I just got an email from Jessica. It's to me and Arthur.

NATALIE What does it say?

NORMAN (*reading aloud*) Dear Daddy and Uncle Norman, I'm writing to express my profound sorrow and disappointment about what's happened to our family in the wake of Grandpa's death . . .

Norman notices Arthur entering and pauses.

Arthur, holding flowers in one hand and his cell phone in the other, is also engrossed in Jessica's email. Norman and Arthur lock eyes for a moment. Then Norman continues:

NORMAN (*still reading*) . . . Most tragedies bring families closer together, but not ours. All we do is fight, and the two of you are the worst offenders. No one's immune from your fallout. Even I got dragged into it. It's not right for brothers to treat each other the way you do.

I'm sure Grandpa would be heartbroken. I know I am . . . Gandhi once said, "You cannot shake hands with a closed fist." I hope you'll both think about that. Please kiss Grandma for me. Love, Jessica.

There's an uncomfortable silence, as Norman contemplates the egg on his face.

Well then . . . If you people will excuse me, I'm going to jump out the window.

ARTHUR Would you mind if I landed on top of you?

NORMAN (*checking out his fist*) I wonder how Gandhi would've felt about the fist bump.

ARTHUR (*also making a fist*) It's a closed fist, yet it's still a shake of sorts.

NORMAN Interesting.

ARTHUR Maybe Gandhi got it wrong.

Then, finally succumbing to their better angels, they bump fists.

ARTHUR (*derisively*) Gandhi . . .

NORMAN   What the hell did he know . . .

Brenda enters, wearing an argyle scarf.

NATALIE   Hi, Mom.

GLORIA (*noticing Brenda*)   Brenda . . . Is that the scarf?

BRENDA (*approaching the bed*)   It is.

GLORIA   It looks lovely on you.

BRENDA   Thank you.

NORMAN (*also approaching the bed*)   Ma, I've got something to tell you. I'm really glad you're okay, but, alas . . . you're going to have to move out. I hope you understand.

GLORIA   Of course I understand. (*laying it on*) I have a cousin in Virginia. She's a raging alcoholic. Maybe she'll take me in. Or I'll go to one of those nursing homes.

ROSE   We would take you, but we have a dog.

NORMAN (*gesturing to Brenda*)   Okay, Stewie. Go ahead.

STEWIE   What?

NORMAN   Tell her you're sorry.

STEWIE   For what?

NORMAN   You know what. Go ahead.

STEWIE   . . . Brenda, I'm really sorry I called you a cunt.

BRENDA   Thank you, Stewie. I appreciate that.

STEWIE   But I still don't know why they didn't have meatballs and spaghetti in that place. It's ridiculous!

Adlibs from all, weighing in on this. Brenda approaches Norman. All is well.

ARTHUR   Mom, I almost forgot. (*he hands her the flowers*)

90

GLORIA   Oooh, Arthur. Flowers. Beautiful.

NORMAN   Really? You used to find flowers depressing. You said they die in two days and that's the end of them.

GLORIA   I'll enjoy them while they last.

ARTHUR   Okay, people, hear me out. As many of you know, I'm a jerk.

Murmured adlibs of agreement from all, ending with:

ROSE   . . . Ever since you were a little kid.

ARTHUR   Fortunately, I have people around who aren't afraid to tell me. It's not true about how it takes a big man to admit a mistake. Small men can do it too. I'm going to make this easy on everybody . . . Mom, I want you to come live with me.

More collective adlibs, this time of approval, except from a sour Norman.

GLORIA   You're serious?

ARTHUR   Never been more serious in my life.

GLORIA   That's so sweet of you, Arthur.

NORMAN   Yes, that is very sweet of you, Toro, but the thing is . . . she's kind of already in my house. She'd have to move. Thanks—very sweet gesture, it means a lot—but we're good.

ARTHUR   Normal, how hard is it to move? I drive up in the van, throw a couple of suitcases in it, and we're off.

NORMAN   I know, but Dad said he wanted me to take care of her.

ARTHUR   No, actually, he didn't. He asked me.

NORMAN   Uh-uh, he was looking right at me!

ARTHUR   Baloney.

NORMAN   Baloney? No, I've thought about this a lot . . .
I remember the moment. He was looking at me.

ARTHUR   You're wrong, Norman. It was me.

NORMAN   No, no. It was me.

ARTHUR   Let's ask Mom.

NORMAN   Okay, let's ask Mom. Mom . . . ?

GLORIA   . . . Not sure. But I can find out. Next time Diego stops
by, I'll ask him.

ROSE   Diego? Who's Diego?

BRENDA   Yeah, who's Diego?

GLORIA   A dear friend . . . A very dear friend.

Curtain

END OF PLAY.